HUNGRY

↗HUNGRY

INTEGRITY®
PUBLISHERS
Nashville

AN ULTRA VERTICAL DEVOTIONAL ADVENTURE

HUNGRY

Copyright © 2003 by Integrity Publishers. Devotions written by Christa Farris.

Published by Integrity Publishers, a division of Integrity Media, Inc., 5250 Virginia Way, Suite 110, Brentwood, TN 37027.

HELPING PEOPLE WORLDWIDE EXPERIENCE *the* MANIFEST PRESENCE *of* GOD.

Unless otherwise indicated, Scripture quotations used in this book are from The Holy Bible, New International Version (NIV). ©1973, 1978, 1984, International Bible Society. Used by permission of Zondervan Bible Publishers.

Other Scripture references are from the following sources: The Message (MSG), copyright ©1993. Used by permission of NavPress Publishing Group.

Cover and Interior Design: The Office of Bill Chiaravalle / www.officeofbc.com

Library of Congress Cataloging-in-Publication Data

Hungry : an ultra vertical devotional adventure.
  p. cm.
ISBN 1-59145-080-2
1. Devotional calendars.
BV4810.H745 2003
249—dc22

2003015139

Printed in the United States of America
03 04 05 06 07 RRD 9 8 7 6 5 4 3 2 1

Presented to: Madeline Peters

From:

Foreword

I think it's hard to really know anyone these days. With pressure on us from all sides to perform in accordance with people's expectations—and with everything from email and instant messaging to tinted SUV windows and Revlon cosmetics as our resources—it's almost as if we're in the business of hiding from one another. I believe that's because when it comes down to it, we don't know who we really are or what we were made for. That's certainly true of me. I would rather disengage than to make a fool of myself. But why is this true of us? How could people living in the Information Age not know something as basic as themselves?

The answer to that question is why this book is so important. We will never truly know ourselves or what we were made for without a true knowledge of God. If we believe there is indeed a God, our first priority should be learning about Him and trying to discover who He really is. But everyone says they know things about God, and many disagree over what they believe. So how can we really know what God is like?

There is only one source that we can trust to point us in the right direction: the Bible. The Bible is God's very words and therefore it's completely trustworthy. Who better to inform the way we think about God than God? In *A New Systematic Theology of the Christian Faith,* Dr. Robert Raymond said, "If men are to know what God is really like, they must turn to God's revelation of Himself in Holy Scripture, where they can behold Him aright." Arthur Pink, another great Christian teacher, said, "The foundation of all true knowledge of God must be a clear mental apprehension of His perfections as revealed in Holy Scripture. An unknown God can neither be trusted, served, nor worshiped." So as you can see, the things we will examine in this book deserve our utmost attention and study, as they go to the very heart of what we believe as Christians.

As we're learning about God's faithfulness, compassion, peace, intimacy, and presence, it would benefit us to try and keep some "Trinitarian" perspective. For such a big word it has a fairly simple intent: Whatever characteristics we learn about and attribute to God the Father, we should also think about in terms of God the Son and God the Holy Spirit. While God is one in "essence," He is comprised of three persons (Father, Son, and Holy Spirit). So as we talk about the compassion of God, we should not only think about how our Father is compassionate, but also the compassion of Jesus. This might prove to be a helpful perspective to carry with us through the book.

Also, we must pray that the Holy Spirit would accompany us on this journey. Only with His guidance can we truly begin to understand something of God's attributes and character.

As you read, you will likely find some familiar language. In fact, you might be surprised at how much of what you experience day to day will show up in these pages. However, since our study is founded on Scripture, we will need the Holy Spirit to rightly interpret for us what we're reading so that we might understand. And we should pray that what we learn might not just inform us, but that it might change us. In Arthur Pink's book *The Attributes of God,* he said, "If the reader is to truly profit from his perusal of the pages that follow, he needs to definitely and earnestly beseech God to bless them to him, to apply His Truth to the conscience and heart, so that his life will be transformed thereby." That is true of this book as well.

As we learn what's true about God, we also begin to see what's true about us. We begin to realize the ways that we were created in His image and, consequently, the glory that we're made for. However, with knowledge as great as this comes great responsibility. In light of this clear teaching of some of God's attributes, we are called to stop hiding from one another and to be those who would throw open our windows and doors to let the fresh air of true biblical community rush in and revolutionize the way we live with and love one another. I pray that God would use this book to glorify Himself to that end.

Derek Webb
Nashville, Tennessee
May 2003

Introduction

In *Bruce Almighty*—a recent flick directed by a believer named Tom Shadyac and starring rubber-faced actor Jim Carrey—Carrey's character, Bruce, learns a few lessons about God's power when he adamantly expresses his rage to his Creator. When Bruce's job as a reporter isn't as glamorous as he hoped, and he continues to face daily frustrations, he's quick to blame his troubles on "the big guy upstairs."

Then, in a crazy twist of movie fate, God grants Bruce an endowment of His power to see how he'd handle the biggest responsibility in the universe. And as expected, Bruce uses his newfound abilities selfishly before realizing that he could really make a difference in people's lives if he chose to.

As believers in Jesus Christ, we realize how absurd the movie's premise is. In Psalm 147:5, the Psalmist says, "Great is our LORD and mighty in power; his understanding has no limit." Certainly, God's limitless understanding isn't going to be translated properly through something as simple as a movie script. Still, this fictional situation reminds us that God's power is something humans can never fully grasp.

Even at his best, Bruce never understands the nature and purpose of God's power. In Ephesians 1:19-20, Paul says his hope for the church was that its people would begin to understand "[God's] incomparably great power for us who believe." Elaborating further, Paul says, "That power is like the working of his mighty strength, which he exerted in Christ when he raised him from the dead and seated him at his right hand in

AN ULTRA VERTICAL DEVOTIONAL ADVENTURE

↗HUNGRY

the heavenly realms." Now that's certainly a far cry from anything we as humans could aspire to.

In the next few pages, we're going to examine more closely five unique facets of God's power and learn about how this attribute fits into the context of His character, has the ability to save us from sin and death, and should lead us down a path to humility.

Insight →

Tim Hughes on God's power

"It brings such hope and strength to me to know that God is all-powerful. Sometimes circumstances lead to that feeling of being out of control—whether it's a health thing or a relationship issue. But just to know that God is all-powerful, and that He's got the whole world in His hands, brings peace and security. I also think that the power of God is such an exciting thing when you see Him coming in and changing lives. I work with a lot of young people and it can take years for people to change, but sometimes God just comes in and breaks things that have held people. Seeing people being healed and God moving in such wonderful ways, it just makes you think, *What an incredible God, that He can do that.*" (For more about this artist, visit CCMMagazine.com)

> *Tim Hughes is an artist on SixSteps Records and a worship leader in the United Kingdom who recently won his first Dove Award for his praise anthem "Here I Am to Worship."*

Unlike Humans, God's Not Power Trippin'

today's verse:

"Now the earth was formless and empty, darkness was over the surface of the deep, and the Spirit of God was hovering over the waters. And God said, 'Let there be light,' and there was light."

Genesis 1:2-3

In most cases, power in today's society is equated with someone's status, clout, or the quality of his/her material possessions. Is the car you drive a junker or a new Jaguar? Is your job a lucrative six-figure career in the corporate world or a minimum-wage gig of grunt-working for the higher-ups? Is your look defined by a pair of Payless sneakers or the latest Prada pumps?

Not that there's anything wrong with owning a nice car or a killer pair of heels, but these superficial status symbols typically figure in to the world's "money is power" perception, and people will often do anything it takes to reach this enviable status. In fact, *Entertainment Weekly* designates one issue each year as the "Power Issue" and ranks all the top names in the biz—from the CEOs of major motion picture companies to bankable movie stars like Reese Witherspoon, Julia Roberts, and Ben Affleck.

If God happened to be included on that list, where do you think He'd rank? Would He crack the top twenty? How about the top ten? Since His immeasurable power goes beyond actual dollars and cents, He'd probably fail to make the cut.

But with God's ability to literally form the world from nothing, no amount of cash, stock options, or star power can even compare. In a world full of get-rich schemes and greed, the Creator of the universe could perpetually be on the ultimate power trip with all He's done. But instead, He carried out the task of creation without much fanfare and changed a lifeless void into a lush planet by merely speaking it into being. The ultimate display of His might began with creation and still continues today as He possesses the power to complete any task, to answer any prayer, to heal, save, and forgive. Not a bad list of accomplishments for a resumé, is it?

HUNGRY

read →

To discover more about God's magnificent power through creation, re-read the full account of creation in Genesis 1-2.

pray →

Now that you've been reminded once again about God's incredible power, let this provide fuel to your prayers. He can accomplish anything! So take some time and pray for those close to you who may not have a personal relationship with Christ yet. Be patient and wait for powerful answers to your prayers—whether it's today, next week, next month, or even later.

write →

Jot down a thought or two about when you've seen God's power poignantly demonstrated in your own life. When times are particularly difficult, use this as a reminder of how His power was evident in your time of need.

apply →

Use something you've learned in today's devotional as a springboard for action in your life. In the same way God uses His power without having to publicize it to the masses, humbly use the power He has given you in your sphere of influence to serve others in a substantial way. You'll be amazed how the combination of God's power and your humility will radically change things.

listen →

"God of Wonders," featuring Cliff and Danielle Young from **Caedmon's Call, Sixpence None the Richer**'s Leigh Nash, and **Third Day**'s Mac Powell from City on a Hill (Essential); "*Great Light of the World"* by **Bebo Norman** from *Myself When I Am Real* (Essential).

HUNGRY

I remember seeing/hearing about God's power in Mexico. when we were running short on beans. After praying over the pot, they seemed to never end.

I also see God's power in nature. Standing at the top of a ski hill or on the edge of the bay at Dryberry I can see how wonderful + creative God is.

Taylor talked about God's power in the way

that he helped her
family throughout their
move, always placing
someone in their lives
that led them back to
a connection with home.

_____

_____

_____

_____

_____

_____

_____

_____

_____

_____

_____

_____

_____

_____

_____

_____

_____

_____

God's Power Is Mysterious Like the X Men, But Absolute

today's verse:

"Your throne, O God, will last for ever and ever; a scepter of justice will be the scepter of your kingdom."

Psalm 45:6

There's something intriguing about the power that fictional superheroes possess. In the recent X Men sequel, *X2: X Men United,* the audience is introduced to a few freakish types who harbor powers ranging from the ability to manipulate fire, to igniting storm clouds with a glassy-eyed stare or morphing seamlessly into the identity of anyone they choose. While far-fetched, superheroes usually are multifaceted—relatively normal folk by day, supercharged assailants at night—and often use their powers in a vigilante attempt to rid society of evil. And it's this good-versus-evil conflict that keeps audiences engaged despite the plot's implausibility. Most people want to see good prevail, but is this the way God would accomplish it?

Even more intriguing than the superheroes is the breadth of God's power. Unlike a mere mortal—fictional or otherwise—God's authority can't be explained by ordinary means. His power is tempered by love. The Bible documents many instances of God's absolute power tempered by mercy.

In Exodus 9, God gave Moses very specific instructions in verses 13-16. He told him to "Get up early in the morning, confront Pharaoh and say to him, 'This is what the LORD, the God of the Hebrews, says: Let my people go, so that they may worship me, or this time I will send the full force of my plagues against you and against your officials and your people, so you may know that there is no one like me in all the earth. For by now I could have stretched out my hand and struck you and your people with a plague that would have wiped you off the earth. But I have raised you up for this very purpose, that I might show you my power and that my name might be proclaimed in all the earth.'" Shortly after that, the Lord sent one of the greatest hailstorms in history.

The interesting thing here is that rather than simply giving people their due (like a superhero might do), the Lord first issued a warning—showing that His power is always balanced with grace and love.

HUNGRY

read →

Other passages elaborating on God's inexplicable power are Psalm 147:5 and Jesus' account on the conflict with the Sadducees in Matthew 22:23-33. For additional insight, check out *The Promise of God's Power: Fresh Encounters with the Living God* (Zondervan) by Jim Cymbala, pastor of the Brooklyn Tabernacle.

pray →

As you reflect on God's power that's balanced with mercy, relate that to your life. Do you treat people with respect even if they don't deserve it? Do you favor wrath over mercy when in situations of power? Ask God to give you His mindset when dealing with difficulties.

write →

While we'll never possess absolute power like God, how can we live a life that models His attribute of balancing power with what seems like an insane amount of mercy?

apply →

Set out to live a superhero-like existence of defending good while keeping God's principle of mercy in the forefront of your mind. Rather than taking a judgmental stance, let love and grace prevail in your confrontational dealings.

insight →

Newsboys' Peter Furler on the power of God

"You see God's power in nature, you see it in adversity, and you see it in funerals. You also see it at weddings, and you see it at football games; it's everywhere. You see plenty of man's power, but God's power is so much more beautiful. It's not an authority that's grasped . . . anytime authority is grasped, it's not really authority at all. Anytime it's forced, it doesn't feel like it's true. His authority doesn't appear to me to be that way." (For more about this artist, visit CCMMagazine.com)

Furler is the frontman for the band, which recently released an album of old and new worship favorites titled Adoration: The Worship Album *(Sparrow).*

HUNGRY

To balance power + mercy give grace.

If we give people grace we model God's characteristics and give people a second chance like he did when he died on the cross!

The Gospel Is God's Own Brand of Electricity

today's verse:

"I am not ashamed of the gospel, because it is the power of God for the salvation of everyone who believes . . ."

Romans 1:16a

At some juncture in your journey with God, you've likely heard or pondered the age-old question: Can God create a rock so heavy that He can't lift it? The mere thought probably boggled your mind. I know it challenged my typically logical way of thinking. After all, if God is omnipotent, surely He could fashion a rock so heavy that He couldn't bear the weight of it. Yet if He did, wouldn't that negate His power to do anything?

The problem with this question is that it assumes "God can do anything." This simply isn't true. God can't lie, for example. God can do only those things that are consistent with His nature and will. In other words, God can do only the things He wants to do. Far more important than creating a big rock is God's desire to save us from our sins. God WANTS to bring us back into fellowship with Him, and He is more than powerful enough to do it!

It's by God's righteousness that we are saved and freed from those overwhelming shackles of sin that separate us from Him. And it's this simple truth that separates Christianity from other faiths. Instead of having to achieve a level of "righteousness" through good deeds or proper behavior of our own, God bestows His righteousness upon us, even though we don't deserve it. His righteousness is liberating and is more than sufficient if we're willing to simply accept it. Yes, one has to receive God's righteousness in the same way you would receive any gift. But it's a leap that results in a rewarding relationship with the God of the Universe, who has the power to save anyone regardless of his or her past.

HUNGRY

read →

Check out Paul's letter to the Ephesians in 1:18-21, where he so eloquently describes just how magnificent God's saving power is.

pray →

With a greater understanding of God's saving power, I encourage you to pray for someone in your family, or a friend, neighbor, or co-worker who doesn't know Jesus as his or her personal Savior. Pray for opportunities to show God's love to that individual so they, too, can experience the power of God through the gospel.

write →

Take a few minutes to write down your testimony. Reflect on the moment when you remember experiencing God's saving power and how that changed your life. Whether that was a week ago or many years in the past, it's good to be reminded of God's tremendous ability to save us from sin and the new creation we are in Him as a result.

apply →

Commit to pray on a daily basis for those who don't have a relationship with Jesus Christ and to love them unconditionally. Be patient if you don't see results right away or don't feel like your efforts make a difference. They do! And who knows, you just may be the catalyst for them to investigate what a relationship with God really entails.

insight →

Avalon's Jody McBrayer on the power of God

"I think there's probably more uncertainty now than there ever has been, at least in my lifetime. In that, it's a comfort for me to know that the power of God is unlimited—that He is in control—and where the power of man fails, desperately sometimes, His power is perfect. We sing a song called "Adonai" every night, and I can't help but think about His power and magnificence. The God who created the entire universe with a single word, He loves us and He cares about us and wants the best for our lives. I'm so thankful He's on our side and that I have that power and security in my life." (For more about this artist, visit CCMMagazine.com)

McBrayer is a vocalist for Avalon, which recently released its greatest hits project titled The Very Best of Avalon: Testify to Love *(Sparrow). McBrayer's first solo effort,* This Is Who I Am *(Sparrow), also hit stores in 2002.*

HUNGRY

- had faith oz a child.
- watched "the Jesus movie"
- asked him into my heart.

- when I was younger sometimes I would feel so sad for no reason. Now I think it is because God was trying to tell me something or I felt others pains very deeply.

- I felt like God used to speak to me thru this event hough I didn't know t.

_____

_____

_____

_____

_____

_____

_____

_____

_____

_____

_____

_____

_____

_____

_____

_____

_____

_____

Jesus—Still Powerful Enough to Be a Miracle Worker

today's verse:

"Then Jesus said, 'Did I not tell you that if you believed, you would see the glory of God?'"

John 11:40

With so many hoaxes and fabricated stories of miracles available as close as your TV set or computer screen, it's often difficult to believe that God is both willing and still powerfully able to perform modern-day miracles.

And even though Mary and Martha spent time with Jesus on a regular basis, it was hard for them to believe when He said their brother Lazarus's "sickness will not end in death." Really, who could blame Mary and Martha? When Lazarus died, the situation looked impossibly bleak. How would Jesus stay true to His word that the sickness wouldn't end in death when Lazarus had already died?

Well, it's likely you know the rest of the story. Jesus raised Lazarus from the dead and, like always, Jesus remained true to His promise.

God's power is still strong, and He still actively performs miracles today —whether they're spiritual needs, physical needs, financial traumas, or broken relationships. If you're familiar with the urban pop sounds of sisters Erica and Tina Atkins-Campbell—more commonly known to Christian music fans as Mary Mary—there's no doubt that you've heard the group's catchy hit "Shackles (Praise You)." Tina says the song addresses the bondage people have in their lives. *"Take the shackles off my feet so I can dance/I just wanna praise Ya, just wanna praise You/You broke the chains, now I can lift my hands/And I'm gonna praise Ya, I'm gonna praise You."*

Yes, God continues to perform miracles today by freeing people from the bondage they experience. Bodies are healed, lives are healed, homes are healed. Perhaps you have experienced some kind of physical or emotional healing, or you know someone who has. Whatever we may have experienced in the way of modern miracles, no miracle compares to the miracle of salvation that Jesus performs every day when people are forgiven and healed of the spiritual disease of sin. If Jesus can save a person from sin, He is certainly able to cure a disease or save a relationship.

HUNGRY

read →

There are so many accounts of Jesus' miracles in the four Gospels that we don't have room to list them all. But let these examples inspire you as you read about Jesus healing a man with leprosy in Matthew 8:1-4, the restoration of a paralyzed man in Mark 2:1-12, and the freeing of a man from demon-possession in Luke 4:33-36.

pray →

You probably don't have to think for too long to come up with someone who needs a miracle in his or her life. Whether it's a neighbor running a little short on rent money or a friend struggling with addictions or a physical illness, your prayers can make a difference.

write →

Use the next few minutes to note where you need a miracle in your life. Be honest, and don't be afraid to jot down exactly what you need. God knows your heart and is more than capable of meeting your needs in any area of your life.

listen →

For great music that fits with today's topic, be sure to check out **Mary Mary**'s latest album, *Incredible* (Integrity), and **Mark Schultz**'s self-titled debut *Mark Schultz* (Word). Also look for the track "Sanctify" from **Delirious**'s CD, *King of Fools (Furious)*.

HUNGRY

I need a miracle in my
attitude towards things.
I sometimes lack joy
and happiness and
therefore motivation.
Not as much anymore
but I also struggle
with bitterness
and resentment and
jealousy. This is
something I believe
God can change in
me if I allow him
and this will also
bring me more happiness.
as for my lack of motivation
and drive, I believe

God can do the
same thing in
me. This in turn
will help me to
not slack off and praise
God in everything
I do.

The Weak Shall Inherit Power

today's verse:

"But he said to me, 'My grace is sufficient for you, for my power is made perfect in weakness.'
Therefore I will boast all the more gladly about my weaknesses, so that Christ's power may
rest on me."

2 Corinthians 12:9

From the statement "The first shall be last," to His promise to "use the foolish things to confound the wise," one of God's most interesting traits is the tendency to do almost everything the opposite of how many of us would approach the same scenario.

Even Christianity itself is a stretch from what's deemed appropriate in society. We're often told from a very young age to pursue the American dream of life, liberty, and happiness that usually includes Mr. or Ms. Right, the trendiest digs, and enough material possessions to keep us from getting bored. But in God's economy, these futile things rarely matter. Believers are instead promised a journey down the unpopular narrow path where life is guaranteed to have trials and where people aren't always going to embrace our beliefs and may, in fact, persecute us as a result.

The apostle Paul knew a thing or two about persecution, having experienced it firsthand. Paul made an interesting declaration in 2 Corinthians 11:30 when he proclaimed, "If I must boast, I will boast of the things that show my weakness." Now seriously, who would want to do that? Why not boast about your talents, wealth, or the loaded SUV you just purchased?

Well, it turns out this statement was made at an interesting juncture in Paul's life. He was hearing great revelations and seeing tremendous visions from the Lord, and to keep from getting haughty about what he was experiencing, he was given "a thorn in his flesh" (something the Bible doesn't specifically identify) to remind him to fully depend on God. Paul learned from this "thorn" that God's strength was made perfect in Paul through his weaknesses.

As Christians, we certainly can take a cue from Paul's experience. When things are going well in our lives—when the bills are paid and all our relationships are solid—we often are confident in our own strength. It's natural to call on God for help in time of need, but are we choosing to boast in our weaknesses and acknowledge God's power even when we're not struggling?

read →

Read 1 Peter 3:8-19. There are some encouraging and relevant verses here that address the topic of how to deal with persecution for doing God's will, and how "it is better, if it is God's will, to suffer for doing good than for doing evil."

write →

It's not easy to completely rely on God's strength in every situation—whether life is smoothly sailing along or incredibly difficult. Use the next few lines as a place to confess which areas are the most difficult to rely on God's power in the midst of your weaknesses.

pray →

Tell God specifically how you want His grace to be sufficient in every area of your life. Give thanks to Him for everything with which He blesses you, especially your weaknesses—and ask Him to use those weaknesses to bring about humility and complete dependence on Him.

listen →

"Needful Hands" by **Jars of Clay** from *Exodus* (Rocketown); "His Strength Is Perfect" by **Steven Curtis Chapman** from *Real Life Conversations* (Sparrow).

HUNGRY

No Need for Power Struggles

today's verse:

> *"No, in all these things we are more than conquerors through him who loved us."*
>
> *Romans 8:37*

When I walked down the aisle in my cap and gown at a large church in Minneapolis, shook the hand of the president of my university, and accepted my journalism degree back in 1998, I assumed my days of vocational struggle were over. No more late nights spent slaving at the college newspaper office writing about tuition hikes. No more interning, where you never quite measure up to the "regular" employees. No more donning my camp uniform while selling tickets for rides at Camp Snoopy at the Mall of America. After all, I was moving to Nashville to accomplish my goal of becoming a writer for a music magazine.

The reality was, like most people right out of college, that my first job wasn't exactly lucrative or exciting. I stuffed envelopes for a living. My boss seemed to get her kicks from making me feel like dirt. She was the one in charge, and I was there for her to boss around. Day after day it got harder to take, but fortunately, I knew it wasn't forever. I ended up staying another two weeks before I quit and accepted another temporary job. Than, a year and a half later, I landed my dream job.

God has complete authority, yet unlike a nagging boss, He never is condescending in the use of His power. In fact, He gives us the power through Him to conquer any difficulty we face. In Romans 8:26, Paul notes, " . . . The Spirit helps us in our weakness. We do not know what we ought to pray for, but the Spirit himself intercedes for us . . ." No matter what we're going through, the Spirit is dutifully praying for us in accordance with God's will. Now that's pretty amazing.

HUNGRY

read →

Read 2 Corinthians 1:3-7. Take a little time this weekend to reflect on these words from Edith Schaeffer, who penned *Affliction* (Ravens Ridge), and consider them as you begin a new week: "No one can really comfort anyone else unless there has been a measure of the same kind of affliction or some kind of suffering which has brought about a deeper understanding, and in which we have ourselves experienced the Lord's comfort."

write →

Now that you've been thinking about God's power for the past several days, write a little about the most compelling, surprising, or intriguing thing you've discovered about God as a result.

pray →

God's power gives us the ability to conquer any difficult situation. Pray about something you're nervous about or an issue that's causing you distress. Know that God will give you the precise amount of strength you need to be and do what He desires. Don't be afraid to ask for it.

listen →

Check out some music this weekend that gives you the opportunity to praise Him as you listen. If you enjoy worship with a modern musical flare, you may want to look for **Michael W. Smith**'s *Worship Again* (Reunion), **Shane Barnard** and **Shane Everett**'s *Carry Away* (Inpop), or **Chris Tomlin**'s *Not to Us* (SixSteps).

HUNGRY

Introduction

The Holiness of God

How can a holy God coexist with sinful humans? How do we follow the call in 1 Peter 1:16 to "be holy, because I am holy" in the choices we make in our daily lives?

The holiness of God is something that's really hard to wrap your mind around; it leads to an abundance of puzzling questions. Holiness is something we can certainly aspire to, yet something we'll never fully attain or even comprehend. After all, only God has the ability to be holy—to be completely set apart from what's sinful and evil.

Before Jesus' time, Moses's brother Aaron had to "present the Levites before the LORD . . . so that they may be ready to do the work of the LORD" (Numbers 8:11). In the customs of their day, people had to be purified before they could approach God, and they were expected to demonstrate God's holiness by their actions. From what they ate to their attire (let's just say that jeans were probably not allowed), the need for holiness and purity permeated everything they did. Contrary to the lives of many modern Christians, these early Israelites were intentional about being separate from the rest of society. They emphasized the need for constant reflection about their sin and were always careful in approaching God.

In our society where we can usually wear whatever we'd like and are free to approach God as a friend because of a personal relationship with Jesus, the need for holiness can

AN ULTRA VERTICAL DEVOTIONAL ADVENTURE

⌐HUNGRY

sometimes get lost. How can we have a life of holiness without succumbing to legalism? How do we live a life of holiness in a society where having moral values is considered taboo? In this week's study, we'll attempt to address some of these questions while learning more about God's holy character.

Insight →

Switchfoot's Jon Foreman on the holiness of God

"A.W. Tozer has an amazing book that I read when I was in college. And that book spun my head around about who God is and His attributes. I think in today's day and age we have this view that we want to put everything in some sort of a cage where it's understandable and convenient. But the holiness of God is something you can never put in a box or fully understand. The mystery of who He is certainly is beyond me, and I think it's good to remember that it's a gift to be able to approach who He is. Yet we will always be continually going deeper and deeper into that mystery. (For more about this artist, visit CCMMagazine.com)

Jon Foreman is the frontman for Switchfoot, whose album The Beautiful Letdown *(Sparrow/Columbia) bowed earlier this year and has garnered hits like "More Than Fine" and "Meant to Live."*

Holy, Holy, Holy—Worshiping with Fervor

today's verse:

"Who will not fear you, O Lord, and bring glory to your name? For you alone are holy. All nations will come and worship before you, for your righteous acts have been revealed."

Revelation 15:4

Whether it's a quarterback lofting a hail Mary pass during those final nail-biting seconds of a football game, or watching The Edge rock out on his trademark guitar lick during "I Still Haven't Found What I'm Looking For" at a U2 concert, it's amazing just how much enthusiasm someone can garner. The sounds of thunderous cheering and shrieks of adoration fill the arena at these events. But when it comes to worshiping the holy Creator of the universe on a Sunday morning, sometimes it sure seems like churchgoers could sing even the numbers in a phone book with more excitement.

As Christians, we can all relate to spiritually dry times. Sometimes it's difficult to get excited about worshiping God. Maybe you had a bad week at work or just had a fight with a boyfriend or girlfriend. Maybe someone in your family is sick with a terminal illness. But it's in these most challenging situations that we need to remember that He still deserves to be glorified and honored, regardless of how we feel. I've often found in the most trying of situations that simply worshiping Him brings a tremendous amount of peace.

During one of her times of struggle, particularly with a bout of writer's block, singer/songwriter Nichole Nordeman sat down and wrote "Holy," a song that was recognized as the Song of the Year at the 2003 Dove Awards. "I knew I'd reached a breakthrough with 'Holy' because it came from such an honest place," Nordeman explains. "It's about my journey away from God and then my prodigal-type return to Him."

When asked why this song has connected with so many listeners, Nordeman comments that many people identify with the song's message of internal spiritual struggle. Having grown up in a Christian home, Nordeman strayed from the faith during college—a period when she felt "enlightened" by various philosophies. "Soon the absolutes of my faith became compromised," she says. Although she wandered away from God, eventually she found herself back where she began. "Many people take the long way around, but then they reach the conclusion that God is holy, and that's all that matters."

HUNGRY

read →

One of the most captivating books I read in one of my college theology classes was *The Holiness of God* by R.C. Sproul (Tyndale House). Like a good suspense novel filled with tremendous twists and turns, we travel with Sproul on his journey to unlock the mystery of God's holiness. He provides many interesting insights on the subject that will really strengthen and challenge your faith.

write →

What does God's holy nature mean to you? Does it cause you to fear God? Does it make Him feel unapproachable? How should knowing that God is holy change your times of personal and corporate worship? Take a moment to scribble down a few thoughts about these topics.

pray →

As you pray today, give thanks that you have the privilege—an all-access pass—to approach God at any time. Because of Jesus, God's holiness does not create a communication barrier between you and Him. Ask that God would give you wisdom as you think more about his attribute of holiness this week.

listen →

You can find **Nichole Nordeman**'s song "Holy" on *Woven & Spun* (Sparrow). Also look for the great duet by **Bebo Norman** and **Cliff & Danielle Young** of **Caedmon's Call** on "Holy Is Your Name" from *City on a Hill: Sing Alleluia* (Essential).

HUNGRY

↗ HUNGRY

The Freedom in Holiness

"But now that you have been set free from sin and have become slaves to God, the benefit you reap leads to holiness, and the result is eternal life."

Romans 6:22

Think of an example of an individual who sets out to lead a "holy" life, and a certain stereotypical kind of person generally pops into most people's minds. Maybe it's a monk who lives in a monastery and dedicates his entire life to prayer, fasting, solitude, and studying the Word. Or it's a pastor who seems so heavenly minded that he causes you to feel like you could never measure up. Or perhaps it's a missionary who has sacrificed a comfortable and familiar life to plod about a distant land in order to share the gospel with the locals.

While all these examples certainly are noble callings that God specifically places upon a person's heart, holiness doesn't require automatic isolation from the rest of the world. When you begin to grasp what God's holiness means, you can't help but respond with a sense of wonder and awe. When you consider that God, who has no connection with sin or evil of any kind, is willing to give "eternal life in Christ Jesus our Lord" (Romans 6:23), you can't help but revel in the freedom that brings. God doesn't call us to embrace holiness because He wants us to obey a certain set of rules. Rather, it's because complete surrender to Him allows us to experience the full-ness of life and the blessings that God has for us.

Surprisingly, people still succeed on a certain level, even when they choose to ignore His plan, but second-best is a long way from God's best. In Genesis, God told Abraham that he would be "the father of many nations." However, when Abraham didn't see immediate results, he took matters into his own hands with Hagar because of his wife's apparent inability to conceive. God still allowed Abraham to be blessed with the birth of Ishmael, but Ishmael wasn't the fulfillment of the ultimate blessing God initially promised. After all, God had told him Sarah would bear the son of promise, not Hagar.

But, in His grace and love, God made another covenant with Abraham and promised that he and Sarah would still have a son—even in their old age. God proved once again that nothing is impossible with Him. Abraham's obedience led to the blessing of a son, Isaac. This example makes me wonder what I might be missing out on because of a lack of patience or respect for God's plan. Ultimately, His plan is always better than anything we dream up for ourselves.

HUNGRY

read →

When we begin to have awe for God's holiness, we fear Him. This fear doesn't mean being scared; rather, it's a healthy, reverential respect. Read more about this in Proverbs 9:10-12.

write →

We talked about how respect for God's holiness leads to freedom. How does that have an impact on your life? What plans has God revealed to you for your life that you've tried to orchestrate your own way? Write and reflect about these specific areas today.

pray →

Ask for wisdom to better understand and grasp His holiness. Ask God which areas of your life He wants to reveal a grand plan for, and be willing to surrender those plans to Him, letting Him carry them out the way He wants instead of trying to make things happen yourself.

insight →

The Rev. Dr. Inderjit Bhogal on the holiness of God

"God's holiness is not seen in God's remoteness or separateness from the stranger, but by God's utter concern for the stranger, by God's adoption and embrace of the stranger. God requires nothing less from those who would be holy. God is outraged when 'the stranger residing among you suffers extortion' (Ezekiel 22:7). This is the God who is seen in Jesus of Nazareth. God is the incarnate one, the one who is with us." (For more about this author, visit CCMMagazine.com)

Dr. Inderjit Bhogal is Director of the Urban Theology Unit in Sheffield, England, and a Methodist minister. In 2000 he was elected president of the British Methodist Conference.

HUNGRY

HUNGRY

A Holy Life in an Unholy World?

today's verse:

"You were taught, with regard to your former way of life, to put off your old self, which is being corrupted by its deceitful desires; to be made new in the attitude of your minds; and to put on the new self, created to be like God in true righteousness and holiness."

Ephesians 4:22-24

First Peter 1:16 charges Christians with a command to "be holy, because I am holy." In a society where most people aren't approaching life with a Christian worldview, are using sex to sell everything from clothes to chewing gum, and often value religious tradition above a relationship with Jesus, how does one aspire to live a life set apart from sin? And how do we balance that with the need to have some connection to popular culture without becoming part of it, or without creating a Christian subculture that alienates us from the rest of society and doesn't allow us to fulfill the Great Commission of making disciples?

As cliché as it may seem sometimes, there's good news despite the weight of the task. God is always with us and has given us the gift of the Holy Spirit to provide discernment and personal "checks" that help us know what's right and wrong. Of course, whether or not we listen to that voice is entirely another matter. The Spirit's guidance is available, and the closer and more frequently we communicate with God in prayer and by reading His Word, the greater our sensitivity will be to His voice.

The bad news is that it's so easy to trip up, which makes us even more thankful that God thoroughly understands our human nature. Forgiveness is available, and every day is a new beginning with a new opportunity to start again. You don't have to be discouraged when you fail because God is ready, willing, and able to forgive. Of course, the more you develop your relationship with God, the less you'll want to do things that grieve His heart.

Living a holy life dedicated to serving Jesus is more than being able to check off a list of do's and don'ts. It's about our hearts becoming more like the heart of God. It's a process of developing a relationship that becomes more and more important to us all the time. We want to be holy because it pleases the One we love and who loves us.

HUNGRY

read →

As we learn more about God's character, it becomes easier to understand why He wants us to be more like Him. Read Psalm 99 for additional insight into God's greatness, holiness, might, and justice.

write →

Thinking about God's holiness can bring a sense of guilt about the areas where you've fallen short. But don't let your thoughts linger in guilt. Rather, confess these weaknesses to God by writing them out.

pray →

Look again at the things you've just written above. Ask God for help in these struggles. He is eager to give you the wisdom you need. Be sure to thank Him as you continue to grow in the quest for personal holiness.

listen →

On **Jennifer Knapp**'s album *Kansas* (Gotee), she poignantly addresses many of the struggles we've talked about today: how to reconcile our sinful nature while serving a holy God. Also check out another CD that will challenge your thinking: **Derek Webb**'s *She Must and Shall Go Free* (INO).

HUNGRY

HUNGRY

Meet the Holy Spirit: One-Third of the Trinity

today's verse:

"… but God has revealed it to us by his Spirit. The Spirit searches all things, even the deep things of God. For who among men knows the thoughts of a man except the man's spirit within him? In the same way no one knows the thoughts of God except the Spirit of God."

1 Corinthians 2:10-11

More than just the conscience of sorts that you envision in cartoon fashion with a devil sitting on one shoulder and an angel on the other, the Holy Spirit is crucial in the discussion of holiness. Get to know more about the Spirit's track record in the crib sheet below:

Crib Sheet

Name: The Holy Spirit, also known as the Comforter, Counselor, the Holy Ghost …

Address: Located in the hearts of those who believe in Jesus Christ

Title: Serves as the third Person of the Trinity

Brief Resumé

The Promised One: In John 14:15-31, Jesus promises the Holy Spirit to His disciples. Verse 17 states, "But you know him, for he lives with you and will be in you."

A Convicting Counselor: In John 16:5-16, Jesus assures His disciples that He will send the Counselor to them, and in verse 8 says, "When he comes, he will convict the world of guilt in regard to sin and righteousness and judgment."

Giver of Life: Romans 8:1-17 addresses how believers have life through the Spirit. In verse 9, it says, "You, however, are controlled not by the sinful nature but by the Spirit, if the Spirit of God lives in you. And if anyone does not have the Spirit of Christ, he does not belong to Christ."

Now that you've learned a few key facts about the Holy Spirit, rest assured that you can go confidently through life with the Spirit, who gives direction, comfort, counsel, and power. We are even more sensitive to God's leading when we're in a vibrant relationship with Him. Knowing God's heart and being attuned to the Holy Spirit are key to facing difficulty and should be things we're aware of at all times.

read →

To learn more about the work of the Holy Spirit, check out Acts, a New Testament book that introduces readers to the apostle Paul and provides an important transition from the story of the life of Christ to the history of the early church.

write →

How have you seen the Holy Spirit work in your life? When has He been your Comforter, Counselor, or Guide in a difficult situation? In your journaling time, consider these questions as you write.

pray →

Ask God for continued sensitivity to His Spirit in your life and the lives of fellow believers in your family, workplace, government, college, or the church as a whole.

insight →

All Star United's Ian Eskelin on the Holy Spirit

"I will never tire of the adrenaline rush [I get] when I'm pouring out my soul and being honest with the crowd," he says. "But at the same time, during that outpouring, I'm being filled up again by the Holy Spirit. It's a really awesome moment." (*CCM Magazine,* January 2003.)

Eskelin has been the frontman for All Star United since the band's inception more than ten years ago. The group's latest effort, Revolution *(Furious), hit shelves last year and garnered plenty of radio airplay with its single "Sweet Jesus."*

↗ HUNGRY

HUNGRY

The Road to Holiness Is Definitely Not Easy Street

today's verse:

"Our fathers disciplined us for a little while as they thought best; but God disciplines us for our good, that we may share in his holiness."

Hebrews 12:10

I've never really enjoyed discipline, but I always have liked its results. When I was a college student, I usually waited until the night before to write every important paper. And every time when I'd be struggling to stay awake while pumping as much coffee and Diet Coke into my body as I could, I vowed I'd never wait until the last minute again. But I did, time and again. Until one time I finally decided not to go the last-minute route, and surprisingly, I felt a lot better about the whole situation. Funny how that happens . . .

Not long ago, my battle with discipline was challenged to gargantuan proportions when I found myself needing to lose a considerable amount of weight. By making good choices at every meal and exercising regularly, I lost even more weight than I had planned in a little more than a year. But discipline was required for those rewarding results. Yet discipline is not always developed easily.

In the same way, spiritual discipline—traveling the road to holiness—is something that doesn't happen overnight. It takes determination, prayer, and a few hits and misses along the way to learn the lessons we need to learn. Unlike many situations in life where the road to success is just a series of tasks you need to accomplish, gaining spiritual discipline is a continuous climb that never reaches the top rung of the ladder.

Fortunately, though, there is hope. In the passage above, we are reminded that God helps us in the discipline process, and He does it "for our good." In Hebrews 12:11, the writer says, "No discipline seems pleasant at the time, but painful. Later on, however, it produces a harvest of righteousness and peace for those who have been trained by it."

 **HUNGRY**

read →

There's a lot of wisdom about spiritual discipline in the Proverbs. Some people read a chapter every day, making their way through the entire book each month. Take a moment and read a few proverbs, and apply that knowledge to your journey to personal holiness.

write →

Focus your attention on the areas where you'd like to grow spiritually. For example, if you'd like to read the entire Bible in a certain amount of time, write that here. If you'd like to dedicate more time to Scripture memorization, note that. Whatever you're hoping to do, set a goal and refer back to this day when you accomplish your goal!

pray →

Ask God to reveal to you where you might need spiritual discipline in your life, and commit to working on that area. When you fall short, don't get discouraged. Every day is a new opportunity to work toward your goal.

listen →

On **Stacie Orrico**'s self-titled album (ForeFront), a couple of songs are relevant to the topic we've just discussed. Check out track two called "(There's Gotta Be) More to Life" and track eight, "I Could Be the One."

HUNGRY

HUNGRY

What We Can Learn from God's Holiness

today's verse:

"May he strengthen your hearts so that you will be blameless and holy in the presence of our God and Father when our Lord Jesus comes with all his holy ones."

1 Thessalonians 3:13

I think today's verse nicely captures the hope, direction, and purpose of this week's study of God's holiness. Like I said in the very beginning, holiness is a difficult issue to consider because our minds aren't capable of fully comprehending something we'll never be. It's a character trait that separates the Creator from the created. Only He is completely holy— blameless and without sin or even a sinful nature, for that matter.

Even without a complete understanding of the concept, we can take comfort in the fact that God's holiness means He'll never lie to us. He'll always be faithful as described in Psalm 89:5. He'll forgive all our sins and heal our diseases like He says in Psalm 103:3, and He's preparing a place in heaven for believers so we can escape eternal separation from God (see John 14:2-3).

It's important to realize that even without the capability of being com- pletely holy like God, we aren't entirely off the hook in the holiness department. In our Christian walk we should take a cue from God's holi- ness and live a life that's pleasing in His sight. Living in accordance with

His plan is always the best way, even though we're able to learn valuable lessons from our mistakes, if we choose to.

As we wrap up this week's study, I want to encourage you to continue on the path to personal holiness. As I wrote this, I was convicted about areas in my life where I could stand to make some better decisions—situations where I could have treated people better or shut my mouth before speaking a harsh word. It's easy for someone writing a devotional to impart challenges to the readers, but it takes humility to admit you have just as many—if not more—faults. So take courage, my friends, as we're all on this journey together. I hope you've enjoyed learning along the way as much as I have.

HUNGRY

read →

Wish you could learn still more about the pursuit of holiness? Jerry Bridges has written a popular book that's sold more than a million copies and contains plenty of practical insight. It's called *The Pursuit of Holiness* (NavPress).

write →

Now that you've been thinking about God's holiness for the past six days, write a little about the most compelling, surprising, or intriguing thing you've discovered about God as a result.

pray →

Ask God to make this week's study about His holiness something that would continue to captivate your heart long after the week is over. Pray that His holiness and faithfulness will inspire you to be more like Him.

listen →

To end the week, look up the words (either in an old hymnal you may have lying around, or use google.com to find them online) to the classic hymn "Holy, Holy, Holy." While it's doubtful that you have a CD that has someone singing it, you probably know the tune and could offer it up as praise to God. It's amazing how much depth and meaning these classic songs have. Listen to the words as you sing it.

HUNGRY

Introduction

If love were represented in the world of fashion, it probably would be something classic—like a great pair of tailored black dress pants or a vintage Levi's jean jacket, because love never goes out of style. From the songs that fill the airwaves of pop radio to the sappy romantic comedies like *Notting Hill* and *Down with Love,* love somehow always figures into the landscape of our lives whether we're looking for it, have lost it, or are completely reveling in it.

Pretty much everyone—whether or not he or she will admit it—longs for that moment when they'll be fully adored, cherished, and romantically swept off their feet complete with candlelight dinners, romantic walks, and genuine affection. If they're not looking for that in life, it's probably because they've been burned before and refuse to be hurt again.

With our society being so incredibly fickle, love between two people isn't always something we can depend on. Human love is often conditional, emotionally driven, and self-serving. When a relationship no longer looks, feels, or acts like we want it to, we're quick to discard it and search for the next option. We seldom want to invest our time in something that needs fine-tuning and doesn't work perfectly right away.

⁊HUNGRY

Fortunately, God's love isn't anything like human love. This week, we're going to investigate this attribute further and learn how God's love is a great model for our relationships, how His love commands us to love one another, and just how His love casts out all fear and covers a multitude of sins. It's a lot to cover in only a week, but I trust this will give you a great springboard for additional study on the topic.

Insight →

Rebecca St. James on the love of God

"Probably the first time I experienced God's love in a very real way was when I became a Christian. I think the next season where I really felt God's love in a very powerful way was when we moved to America and my dad lost his job soon after we moved. We went through real hard times as a family financially, but it was an amazing, spiritually growing time. Unfortunately, I think we grow the most through trials and pain. It would be nice if it happened another way, but I think most of the time real spiritual growth happens through pain. We didn't have a car or furniture, were sleeping on the floor, and didn't know where the next meal was going to come from. But we prayed about everything and saw God do total miracles. People would show up at our house with groceries and furniture. One family gave us a car the same day they met us. God even provided Christmas presents one year. That just made me really passionately experience His love and fall deeper in love with Him." (For more about this artist, visit CCMMagazine.com)

A national spokesperson for abstinence and a member of the Presidential Prayer Team, artist Rebecca St. James recently released a greatest hits project called Wait for Me: The Best from Rebecca St. James *(ForeFront).*

God's Love—More "Forever" than Diamonds

today's verse:

"How great is the love the Father has lavished on us, that we should be called children of God! And that is what we are! The reason the world does not know us is that it did not know Him."

1 John 3:1

The marketing for diamond engagement rings is really nothing short of brilliant. Like an old black-and-white movie, the camera zooms in on the handsome man pulling the perfect diamond ring out of his pocket to present to his beautiful, unsuspecting girlfriend. He opens the box. She gasps in surprise. He slides the sparkling diamond on her finger. They kiss, the music swells, and the ad copy proclaims: "A diamond is forever."

A cynic would say, "Who cares? Their relationship will end a few months after they get married anyway." Meanwhile, the hopelessly romantic majority will begin dreaming of their "forever" moment. Fortunately, the love of our heavenly Father isn't as fleeting and is more forever than most diamonds will ever be.

For many of us, the first part of today's highlighted passage in 1 John is familiar . . . God proclaims the magnitude of His love for us in that He would call us His children. Notice the exclamation marks for added emphasis. He's trying to get our attention with this amazing promise. But something equally intriguing is the part of the verse that you don't often hear. The second part states, "The reason the world does not know us is that it did not know Him." God's love is so different from anything the world can offer that the world is simply unable to recognize or understand it, even when that love is demonstrated in our lives.

Later in the book John adds, "Whoever does not love does not know God, because God is love" (1 John 4:8). How reassuring and wonderful it is to know that the holy Creator of the universe is the literal representation of love! And despite the fact that we continually disappoint Him and fall short of His hopes and dreams for our lives, His love for us is consistent and unchanging.

This promise is something we can rely on when everything seems to be going wrong, when we're feeling antisocial or sad, or when we happen to offend someone by saying the wrong thing at precisely the wrong time. None of those surface issues matter to God because His love is unconditional. Now isn't that comforting to know?

HUNGRY

read →

For extra insight on just how much our heavenly Father loves us, look for Brennan Manning's groundbreaking book *Abba's Child: The Cry of the Heart for Intimate Belonging* (NavPress).

write →

How does the reality that "God is love" affect how you live your life? How does it impact the way you respond to the people with whom you interact on a daily basis? How have you seen God's unconditional love work in your own life?

pray →

Lift up the people in your circle who have yet to know and experience God's love in their lives. Pray that the love of God that lives in you will shine brightly so they might want to seek out what's different about you.

listen →

If you find yourself feeling discouraged, be encouraged in His love by checking out "Smile at Life Again" by **The Elms** from *Truth, Soul and Rock 'n' Roll* (Sparrow) or "The Love I Know" by **PFR** from *Goldie's Last Day* (Sparrow).

HUNGRY

⬈HUNGRY

There's No Need Ever to Be Scared

today's verse:

"There is no fear in love. But perfect love drives out fear, because fear has to do with punishment. The one who fears is not made perfect in love."

1 John 4:18

Like many young children growing up, I often had irrational fears of monsters lurking in my bedroom closet while I tried to fall asleep. Any shadow that would surface on the wall would quickly fuel my anxiety, but I always believed that as long as my mom or dad was home, I really had nothing to worry about because they could zap away the monsters in an instant. While I wasn't quite sure how they would defend me against my imaginary foes, I was completely secure that my parents could and would, exactly when I needed their help, for I knew my parents loved me and didn't want me to be harmed by evil monsters.

In the same way, our heavenly Father—God Himself—wants us to live a life without fear. Whether it's the fear that He won't provide what we need in a crisis or our fear about what the future may hold from an eternal perspective, He wants us to be fully confident that He is there and will always come to our rescue when we need Him.

In Eugene Peterson's translation of the Bible called *The Message,* he renders 1 John 4:16-18 in this way: "When we take up permanent residence in a life of love, we live in God and God lives in us. This way, love has the run of the house, becomes at home and mature in us, so that we're free of worry on Judgment Day—our standing in the world is identical with Christ's. There is no room in love for fear. Well-formed love banishes fear. Since fear is crippling, a fearful life—fear of death, fear of judgment—is one not yet fully formed in love."

Even though God is completely holy, the infinite Creator of the universe, and the final Judge of all humanity, He's also more gentle and loving than the best earthly father. And for those who may not have had the best parental upbringing, it's assuring to know that He'll be the best father you've ever had because He's completely faithful. He is your Provider and loves you more than anyone ever will. So in the same way I trusted my earthly father to fight off imaginary monsters in my room, my heavenly Father is well-equipped to handle the real enemies and difficulties I will have in my lifetime. Now there's a reason for rejoicing!

HUNGRY

read →

Relating to the topic of fear, the Gospel of John, chapter 14, gives an expanded look at why we should never fear when we've received Jesus as our personal Savior.

write →

What are you afraid of? What are you needing to surrender to God's care—to the One who loves you completely? Reflect on a time when God helped you in a time of need and jot down just how He met your need in that particular situation. The next time you're fearful, remember what you wrote here, and let that encourage you.

pray →

Think about the words of the song "Jesus Loves Me" and confess where you're weak and need Him to be strong. Tell Him what's bothering you, and don't be afraid to be candid about it. God certainly can handle any concern you may have. When He answers your prayers, don't forget to write that down as a constant reminder of His faithfulness.

insight →

TobyMac on the love of God

"I think to walk in awareness of His love would be the key aspect for me. I know His love is there, and my wife, Amanda, even tells me, 'You just sort of know God loves you; you know He's gonna take care of you.' And she's like, 'In one sense, it's a very interesting faith walk that you have,' because Amanda's much more intimate with God than I am. But she's like, 'It's a cool faithfulness that you have because you know He loves you and you just live.' I guess it's a compliment. I think for me, it's walking in awareness of His love. Like, I can know He loves me, but there are moments when I'm very aware. And it's weird . . . why does it take sad times, hard times—and if you're really sensitive to God, the best of times—to understand that?" (For more about this artist, visit CCMMagazine.com)

TobyMac is an artist, producer, record label owner, father, advocate for urban music and racial unity, and one-third of one of Christian rock's most successful bands: dc Talk. He recently released a remix album of songs from his solo debut, Momentum *(ForeFront).*

HUNGRY

HUNGRY

God's Always a Team Player

> *"No one will be able to stand up against you all the days of your life. As I was with Moses, so I will be with you; I will never leave you nor forsake you."*
>
> Joshua 1:5

While Moses made his share of mistakes like anyone else, Joshua still had some pretty big leadership shoes to fill when Moses died. After years of toiling, the Israelites were finally about to make their way into the Promised Land. In Joshua 1:7, God instructed Joshua to "be strong and very courageous. Be careful to obey all the law my servant Moses gave you; do not turn from it to the right or to the left, that you may be successful wherever you go."

I don't know about you, but even though Joshua had such clear direction from God, I still probably would've been fearful that I'd mess things up somehow. After these people had waited for such a long time, how would I be able to lead them? Fortunately, Joshua heeded God's word and led the people despite difficult circumstances, including crossing the Jordan River in rather dramatic fashion after it flooded. In the study notes of *The Student Bible* (Zondervan), writers Philip Yancey and Tim Stafford say, "Whatever means God used to allow the Israelites to cross, this miracle echoed the crossing of the Red Sea 40 years before, helping to establish Joshua as a worthy successor to Moses." Now that's pretty incredible.

While it may be without some of the drama of the Joshua account, God shows the same love to us daily by never leaving or forsaking us either. Even in the darkest hours of our lives, He is there to protect, lead, and comfort. No matter what we're going through, we can ever rest assured that God is always on our team and will give the precise instructions we need to accomplish any task He sets before us.

If God could help Joshua lead the Israelites to the Promised Land, He certainly is able to do the impossible through us if we're willing to wait for His lead and listen for His instructions.

read →

The Bible is full of many inspiring accounts of God helping people do what seemed impossible. Skip forward to Judges and read chapter 7 where Gideon defeated the Midianites.

write →

What seemingly impossible tasks do you need God's divine intervention to accomplish? Do you believe He's more than able to help? Use the next few minutes to comment on what you've read today and how you plan to utilize that knowledge in a practical way in your life.

pray →

God assures us that He'll never leave or forsake us. Ask God for the confidence to believe that truth every day—even when situations look grim or impossible.

listen →

As a reminder that God will always be there for you, listen to **Stacie Orrico**'s "Security" from *Stacie Orrico* (ForeFront) or "The Father's Song" by **Matt Redman** from *The Father's Song* (Worship Together).

HUNGRY

HUNGRY

You Want Me to Love Who?

today's verse:

"But I tell you: Love your enemies and pray for those who persecute you, that you may be sons of your Father in heaven."

Matthew 5:44-45

Whether it's at work, at school, or during an annual visit to that pesky family reunion, there's always that one person who pushes your buttons, challenges your normal ability to be nice, and may even torment you to the point where you consider him or her an "enemy." Then there are those for whom you have a genuine dislike. Perhaps it's someone who doesn't like you. Maybe they've offended you or someone you love. In any case, it seems to be unavoidable: There will be people in our lives we simply don't like.

Rather than treating such "enemies" in the manner they've chosen to treat us, God teaches us to be different. It's another lesson about His extravagant love. He asks us not only to pray for the people who get under our skin, but demands that we love them as well. He asks us to do something that isn't always easy—something where we have to rely on His strength in order to succeed. Instead of looking out for "number one," as society would suggest, we have to do what's considered unpopular and humble ourselves even when we feel we are not at fault.

So what's the incentive for going out of our way to love the unlovable? There doesn't need to be an incentive. Knowing that God desires it is incentive enough, but Jesus does provide a reason. In Matthew 5:46-48, Jesus says, "If you love those who love you, what reward will you get? Are not even the tax collectors doing that? And if you greet only your brothers, what are you doing more than others? Do not even pagans do that? Be perfect, therefore, as your heavenly Father is perfect."

Again, this answer defies what seems reasonable or fair—yet this is how God chooses to respond to us. When we don't deserve anything but death and punishment for our sin, God is always waiting for us with opens arms and always willing to forgive—no matter how many times we've made the same mistake. That's the approach He commands us to use when our "enemies" push the boundaries of what seems fair. We're still called to love. It would seem that God is calling us to a higher standard. It's a standard of unconditional love set by His own love for you and me.

HUNGRY

read →

The challenge presented in today's devotional is far from an easy one. It's not part of our human nature to love those who don't always treat us with respect. In Matthew 6:9-13, Jesus gave us the model for prayer. Read these verses several times.

write →

Who is someone (or maybe there's more than one person) in your life who's difficult to love? Write down the name of that person and commit to praying for and treating him or her with extra kindness this week. In my experience of doing this at different junctures in my life, these people eventually became my friends later on. Isn't it funny how God works sometimes?

pray →

See the "Write" section above for your prayer tip of the day.

insight →

Glassbyrd's Mark Byrd on the love of God

"The greatest display of God's love is in the Cross. God entered into our broken and fallen humanity to redeem us. Following His example, we are to be vessels of His love by entering into the suffering of others." (For more about this artist, visit CCMMagazine.com)

Mark Byrd is the co-writer of the popular worship hit "God of Wonders" and used to play in a Christian rock band called Common Children before joining forces with his wife, Christine Glass, to form Glassbyrd. The group's debut Open Wide This Window (Word) released in 2003.

HUNGRY

HUNGRY

Giving Us Hope to Carry On

> *today's verse:*
>
> "For God so loved the world that he gave his one and only Son, that whoever believes in him shall not perish but have eternal life."
>
> *John 3:16*

Today's verse is probably one of the first Bible passages you ever memorized. It's probably even your first thought at the mere mention of the book of John. Despite the verse's familiarity, there's real life-changing power in those twenty-six words.

Those words can lead to eternal life and freedom for someone who hears them. They also poignantly demonstrate the extent of God's love for us: He sacrificed his Son so that we sinful humans could have an opportunity for salvation. It's an amazing, extravagant gift He's given—something we're often so excited to share when we first become a Christian. Like many gifts we receive throughout our lives, however, the enthusiasm often fades when something else makes its way into the spotlight. Nevertheless, God's love for us allows second chances and the privilege of having an intimate relationship with Him as described in Psalm 25:14, "The LORD confides in those who fear him; he makes his covenant known to them."

Unlike many human relationships that waver from day to day, God's covenant with us is constant and consistent. We always can know exactly what to expect from God's love. After all, God is Love. Loving is His nature. His love for us is as constant as He is.

First Corinthians 13:4-8 details all the things that love involves. Love is patient, kind, and lacking envy and the tendency for boasting or behaving rudely. It's also not self-seeking, easily angered, or a list-keeper of wrongs. " . . . Love does not delight in evil, but rejoices with the truth. It always protects, always trusts, always hopes, and always perseveres. Love never fails."

This is how God loves us. It is His constant love that gives us hope to carry on when we become discouraged and grieved. When we are lonely, He is present. When we are sad, He is encouraging. When we are grieving, He is comforting. When we stray, He is guiding us. When we feel unlovely, He is loving. When we lose hope, He is our hope.

HUNGRY

read →

First Corinthians 13 provides us with a great model of how we should approach our friendships, dating relationships, and even our future or present marriage relationships. You can learn even more about how we should love by checking out The Five Love Languages series by author Gary Chapman (Northfield).

write →

What aspect of God's love stands out to you the most? How can you incorporate more of that into your own relationships?

pray →

Ask God to help you love like He loves you. Whether you find yourself being impatient with others, having difficulty trusting people, or dealing with any other interpersonal issue, God is able to help you in your weaknesses. Commit to pray about these struggles today and give thanks for the areas that are a little easier for you.

listen →

There are so many great songs that brilliantly convey the love of God. For starters, **Jars of Clay**'s "I Need You" from *The Eleventh Hour* (Essential) captures our need for God's love. Also, **Sixpence None the Richer**'s "Melody of You" from *Divine Discontent* (Warner Bros. Christian/Reprise) is a poetic, melodic love song aimed squarely at God that declares we belong to Him.

HUNGRY

HUNGRY

Practical Advice for Loving Others

today's verse:

"Above all, love each other deeply, because love covers over a multitude of sins."

1 Peter 4:8

In 1 Peter 4, there are a lot of helpful commands directed at believers to aid in our journey of living for God. In verse 2, we're encouraged to live for the will of God instead of earthly desires. Then, in verse 7, we're told, "The end of all things is near," and are encouraged to be "clear-minded and self-controlled so that you can pray."

Then, just a verse later, the focus switches to how we should respect our fellow man. In the same way that God forgives and still loves us when we fall short, He desires that we love each other extravagantly despite flawed behavior, because "love covers over a multitude of sins."

In the next verse, He takes this call to love to a practical level when we're commanded to "offer hospitality to one another without grumbling." It's amazing sometimes just how God knows our hearts completely. How many times have we welcomed guests into our homes with little enthusiasm, but have done it because it's the *expected* thing to do? That's certainly been the case for me when I've had guests stay during very busy, perhaps even inconvenient, times in my life. And I certainly grumbled plenty, making me the less-than-desirable host that I'm called to be.

Before diving into several verses about suffering for being a Christian, the section ends with the encouragement to the reader to "use whatever gift he has received to serve others, faithfully administering God's grace in its various forms." Until our love becomes practical and finds expression in our actions toward others, it is not a love like God's. His love is active, and He expects our love to be active as well.

Indeed, this is no small task; yet it serves as the perfect place to end our look at the love of God. During the past six days I hope you learned or were reminded just how much love God has for you. In turn, the love He bestows on you is something you need to extend to those around you— to believers as well as unbelievers—so everyone may fully experience the abundant love of our heavenly Father and a relationship with Jesus Christ our Savior.

HUNGRY

read →

To conclude our theme on the love of God, check out the passage on love in 1 John 4:19-21.

write →

Now that you've been learning about the attribute of God's love for the past six days, write a little about the most compelling, surprising, or intriguing thing you've discovered about God as a result.

pray →

Pray for opportunities to demonstrate God's love to people in practical ways. Whether it's meeting physical needs like giving money or baked goods, or time spent helping in a variety of capacities, set out to use your talents to serve others. You'll be amazed at how much you'll be blessed and be a blessing as a result of your generosity.

insight →

Author Brennan Manning on the love of God

"We don't know the love of God except in a vague, distant, abstract way. We don't really believe that God loves us just as we are, not as we should be. He loves us. Not just the guy next to us, not just Billy Graham—He loves us." (For more about this author, visit CCMMagazine.com)

Manning, 70, has penned a variety of books on the subject of God's love during the course of his career and was recently featured in an in-depth story in the May 2003 issue of CCM Magazine.

HUNGRY

Introduction

The Knowledge of God

It's fascinating when we consider just how unique God's creation is, especially when it comes to people. Have you ever thought about just how interesting and diverse our personal preferences are? Why is it that some people enjoy eating meat while others prefer to go the mostly vegetarian route? Or why is one person attracted to buying a lime green-colored car while most people wouldn't give it a second thought? What is it that makes someone attracted to brunettes rather than blondes? While all these examples are simply a matter of our likes and dislikes, it's fascinating how God created each of us with unique personalities and preferences that distinguish us from each other.

When we say we know someone really well, like a friend or someone in our family for instance, we mean we're intimately familiar with the person's preferences, good and bad habits, and the little quirks that set them apart. God knows each of us in the same way we know our moms, dads, siblings, significant others, and best friends. Except with God, the knowledge He has of us is much more in-depth and specific. He knew us before we were created and He has a running count of every hair on our head. He knows exactly what we need . . . and when we need it, right down to the wisdom we require in every situation. In His knowledge He's also fully aware of all our deeds—the good and the bad.

↗ HUNGRY

God's knowledge isn't limited to just people. He knows everything there is to know about everything else as well. From the deepest point in the ocean to the most distant location in the universe, God knows it all. Nothing surprises Him or sneaks up on Him. It's hard to imagine that God's knowledge is infinite, but it is, and understanding that brings us comfort that the universe is not spinning out of control.

How well do we know God, and what does the attribute of the knowledge of God teach us about Him? These are all issues we'll venture into in this week's study focusing on the knowledge of God.

Miss Cleo Never Had a Chance!

"The eyes of the LORD are everywhere, keeping watch on the wicked and the good."

Proverbs 15:3

It's interesting to note just how much we humans crave knowledge—especially when it relates to issues we often have no control over, like what's going to happen in the future. Will we finally meet and marry Mr. or Ms. Right, and when will that be? Will we secure that new job we've applied for and be able to buy our dream house in the suburbs in the next year? Will we stay healthy and safe from harm's way?

The fact that we constantly contemplate questions like these is probably why TV ads featuring psychics like Miss Cleo are so popular, despite their less-than-perfect results. We crave knowledge. We want to know what is going to happen so we can have an edge or prepare somehow for what's coming. We live in an information age where knowledge is power, and we want all we can get!

Thankfully, as Christians we serve a God who is omniscient—a fancy word for "all-knowing." We never have to speculate about His range of intelligence or reliability because He's the Creator of knowledge and is aware of everything that has happened, is happening, and will happen.

As we get to know more about God and are able to recognize and acknowledge His ways, the less we're going to be concerned about the future because we know His track record: We know from His character and our experience that He has everything safely in His capable hands. In the times we're worried, we can always communicate our fears to Him through prayer because He understands our worries as well. Nothing is beyond His knowledge.

Understanding the knowledge of God should provide believers with peace and liberation because God's knowledge supersedes anything we could ever imagine. Yet He's patient and understands why we don't just blindly accept what He has to say. We not only serve a Creator who's smarter than all of the most recognized scholars, but who also has complete control of the universe and rules it with power, patience . . . and love.

HUNGRY

read →

Solomon is considered the wisest man in history, yet all his knowledge didn't necessarily lead to a peaceful life. Read more about his life in the book of 1 Kings.

write →

How does the knowledge that God is all-knowing bring peace in your life? Jot down a few thoughts on that subject as you journal today.

pray →

In our complicated, fast-paced, confusing society, the gift of discernment is a critical thing to have. Like Solomon, pray that God will give you wisdom as you make important decisions today.

listen →

"Twilight" by **Shaun Groves** (Rocketown) and "Wrecking Ball" by **Jill Phillips** (Fervent).

HUNGRY

HUNGRY

God's Into the Details

today's verse:

"My frame was not hidden from you when I was made in the secret place. When I was woven together in the depths of the earth, your eyes saw my unformed body. All the days ordained for me were written in your book before one of them came to be."

Psalm 139:15-16

Isn't it cool to know that God knew every detail about us long before we were born? Before ultrasound testing existed, God knew who our parents would be and orchestrated the growth process of every person in the entire human race. In my case, He knew I'd be born on January 2 in Madison, Wisconsin, would have brown eyes, dark hair, a tall frame, and long, skinny feet.

Psalm 139:13-14 says, "For you created my inmost being; you knit me together in my mother's womb. I praise you because I am fearfully and wonderfully made; your works are wonderful, I know that full well." It's amazing how King David had such awe and reverence for God's incredible handiwork. Not many of us would claim to be "wonderfully made." Rather than focusing on the beauty, complexity, and uniqueness of God's creation, we candidly pick apart our perceived flaws with a fine-toothed comb. We seldom embrace the glory and goodness that God created in us. Reading this passage should be the best boost of self-esteem we've ever received.

God's knowledge means that we are not mere accidents of an evolutionary process. He KNEW what He was doing! He KNEW you before you were born! You may feel like an accident, but you weren't. God knew everything about you before you were ever conceived. You are no accident. And you are "wonderfully made."

Beyond knowing us throughout the creation process, God also knows exactly when our lives will end. I can't speak for you, but I never paid a lot of attention to the latter part of today's verse: "All the days ordained for me were written in your book before one of them came to be." Our Creator already knows what the final day on our tombstones will be. While that may seem morbid to some, and a challenge to live life to its fullest for others, that fact brings me great security. I don't have to worry about death or when it will happen because God, in His infinite knowledge, has it all under control, which is liberating.

The attribute of God's knowledge complements what we talked about last week: the love of God. He knows us and still loves us! He knows where we've been, what we've done when no one's been watching . . . yet loves us completely. Isn't that what we long for? Someone who knows us completely, but still loves us?

read →

Jeremiah chapter 1 is a passage that uses some of the same language as Psalm 139. Read the chapter and learn more about the beginning of the life and "call" for service of one of God's most reluctant servants.

write →

In the Scripture we read today, it says we are fearfully and wonderfully made. Use the space below to write down some of your favorite personal, emotional, and spiritual attributes that God has blessed you with. After writing them down, be sure to give thanks for them.

pray →

In your prayer time today, pray the words that David wrote in Psalm 139:23-24 and take them to heart when God begins to reveal things to you. "Search me, O God, and know my heart; test me and know my anxious thoughts. See if there is any offensive way in me, and lead me in the way everlasting."

insight →

Skillet's Korey Cooper on the knowledge of God

"God, in His sovereignty and wisdom, has placed me here for such a time as this. I want the presence of God to be overflowing in my life; I want to be completely humble and dead to self; and I want to see the tangible presence of God transforming lives and consequently transforming our society." (CCM Magazine, September 2001)

Korey Cooper is one-fourth of the popular rock act Skillet and is married to lead singer John Cooper. At press time, the band was working on a brand new album for Ardent Records, set to hit shelves in late-September 2003.

HUNGRY

HUNGRY

Pray without Mincing (Words, that Is)

today's verse:

"And when you pray, do not keep on babbling like pagans, for they think they will be heard because of their many words. Do not be like them, for your Father knows what you need before you ask him."

Matthew 6:7-8

Unlike certain politicians and high-paid celebrities, one of the most surprising things about God is that He doesn't want our empty flattery or flowery language when we approach Him. Considering how powerful, holy, and knowledgeable He is, it's incredible that all He wants from us is our sincerity. The reason we can bypass the facades with Him is because He already knows what we're going to ask. He knows our hearts and our concerns, and is fully aware of exactly what we need anyway. He just enjoys having a conversation with us and hearing our prayers.

In Matthew 6:25-27, He uses an analogy from nature that frees us to boldly approach Him with everything and that should make it clear that our needs will not go unnoticed. "Therefore I tell you, do not worry about your life, what you will eat or drink; or about your body, what you will wear. Is not life more important than food, and the body more important than clothes? Look at the birds of the air; they do not sow or reap or store away in barns, and yet your heavenly Father feeds them. Are you not much more valuable than they? Who of you by worrying can add a single hour to his life?"

It's comforting to know that God isn't a pretentious ruler who demands that we jump through spiritual hoops to gain access to Him. Instead, God approaches everything with love and is always available to provide wisdom exactly when we need it. At the end of Matthew 6, in verses 33-34, God gives us some great advice—and some great reassurance as well: "But seek first his kingdom and his righteousness, and all these things will be given to you as well. Therefore do not worry about tomorrow, for tomorrow will worry about itself. Each day has enough trouble of its own."

↗ **HUNGRY**

read →

Another model for presenting our requests to God is presented in Matthew 7:7-8 when God tells us to ask, seek, and knock. Read these verses and use this approach when presenting your prayers to God.

write →

Write down some of the barriers that have kept you from spending time in conversation with God in the past. If you have a few extra moments, scribble down some questions you'd ask God, and don't be afraid to present them to Him the next time you pray.

pray →

See "Read" for today's prayer suggestion.

listen →

Because today's lesson was a reflection of God's all-knowing character and a call for us to be sincere when approaching Him, why not listen to some contemplative music to end the study? Check out the new collection of the late **Rich Mullins**'s work called *Here in America* (Reunion) or **Andrew Peterson**'s latest, *Love and Thunder* (Essential).

HUNGRY

⬈HUNGRY

Wisdom—Not Just for Brainiacs

today's verse:

"To the man who pleases him, God gives wisdom, knowledge and happiness, but to the sinner he gives the task of gathering and storing up wealth to hand it over to the one who pleases God. This too is meaningless, a chasing after the wind."

Ecclesiastes 2:26

When it comes to wisdom, many people are quick to assume it's something only reserved for the smart, savvy types who revere great thinkers like Aristotle and Einstein, or who understand the works of avant garde artists and poets like da Vinci and Shakespeare. The book of James quickly dispels that notion in chapter 1, verses 5 and 6: "If any of you lacks wisdom, he should ask God, who gives generously to all without finding fault, and it will be given to him. But when he asks, he must believe and not doubt, because he who doubts is like a wave of the sea, blown and tossed by the wind."

Proverbs also supports the idea that anyone can be wise, and even goes as far as to say that wisdom isn't merely comprised of complex notions. Wisdom is also practical, down-to-earth, and teaches you how to live a meaningful life. In Proverbs 2:1-6, the writer addresses the moral benefits of wisdom. "My son, if you accept my words and store up my commands within you, turning your ear to wisdom and applying your heart to under-standing, and if you call out for insight and cry aloud for understanding, and if you look for it as for silver and search for it as for hidden treasure, then you will understand the fear of the LORD and find the knowledge of God. For the LORD gives wisdom, and from his mouth come knowledge and understanding."

Once again we learn that, true to God's character, He bestows and makes blessings available to everyone, not necessarily just the people you'd expect to be "deserving" of such an honor. Wisdom is available for those willing to listen and be humble, and who trust Him enough to ask for such an extravagant gift.

HUNGRY

read →

To further investigate the Proverbs' insight on wisdom, check out the following passages: Proverbs 1:7; 2:5-9; 8:22-31; 9:10; 22:17-19.

write →

In what areas of your life could you really use the blessing of wisdom? If you've ever been intimidated to ask for this gift, let today's devotional insight make you bold: Approach God for exactly what you need.

pray →

Ask God to reveal the areas of your life in which you need wisdom. Whether it's for financial matters, direction for future endeavors, or any minute daily task, be open to what new, exciting plans He may have for you in the coming months.

insight →

Michael Tait on wisdom he learned from his late father

"Musically, he taught me, 'Don't get caught up in it.' He always said, 'The most dangerous position in the world is to be a Christian singer because you have all the praise coming at you, but you have to be reflectors; you have to give it back to God.' That's something that Grammys can't get you, platinum records can't get you, all the freakin' money in Solomon's temple can't get you. That's what a father does. He passes along wisdom. Those are the jewels." (*CCM Magazine,* May 2001)

Michael Tait is the frontman for Tait, his solo venture outside of dc Talk. The band is planning a sophomore follow-up to Empty (ForeFront) for November 2003.

↗HUNGRY

↗HUNGRY

God Knows Our Deeds

today's verse:

"Do not keep talking so proudly or let your mouth speak such arrogance, for the LORD is a God who knows, and by him deeds are weighed."

1 Samuel 2:3

When you realize that God knows everything, it changes the face of things that the world might consider harmless.

During my junior year of high school, my friend Melissa and I decided to do something good for humanity by organizing a fast at our school. We dutifully promoted the festivities, collected donations, and volunteered to go without food for thirty hours that particular weekend. To make up for our inability to snack, we thought we'd just rent some videos and have a fun night. Thirty hours was just six more than a day; surely we could exercise that small amount of self-control.

With our donations mailed to the headquarters earlier that week and plenty of videos to watch, we were set for Friday. I went over to Melissa's house, and her Mom was making pizza. It smelled great, but we had made a promise. No pizza for us. A few hours later, her family went to sleep and we put a video in. On our way to the kitchen to get some water (surely drinking water wasn't breaking the fast), we spotted a bag of Cool Ranch Doritos on the counter, along with half of the uneaten pizza from a few hours earlier. It looked so good . . . And how could someone really be expected to watch videos without snacks? It seemed inhumane. Before we knew it—only four hours into our fast—we were munching away on Doritos, pizza, and soft drinks.

We didn't feel guilty until we went back to school and our pledgers checked up on us. "Of course it went well; it was so easy," I found myself saying as Melissa smiled and agreed. The lies were brilliant, and our peers admired our dedication.

To some people, it may seem silly to get worked up over something like that, but afterwards I really felt bad about deceiving everyone. Although I didn't feel bad enough to do anything about it. While most everyone likely has a similar story that's humorous to tell in hindsight, taking credit for something you didn't do is a sin. Like it says in today's verse, "for the LORD is a God who knows."

HUNGRY

read →

Check out the context for today's verse by reading all of Hannah's prayer in 1 Samuel 2:1-36.

write →

In what ways have you been less than honest about your actions? Can you think of a time when it really troubled you? If so, how did you reconcile the situation? Is there something you need to do about it now? Write about that here.

pray →

Ask God to make you always sensitive to the Holy Spirit's conviction in your life—even in the small things. Ask Him to show you if there are actions you need to take to deal with a past sin.

listen →

For an honest look into the joys and struggles of life as a Christian, check out **Jaci Velasquez**'s new CD, *Unspoken* (Word).

HUNGRY

HUNGRY

God's Knowledge Is Too Lofty to Attain

today's verse:

"What is more, I consider everything a loss compared to the surpassing greatness of knowing Christ Jesus my Lord, for whose sake I have lost all things. I consider them rubbish, that I may gain Christ."

Philippians 3:8

While we've learned this week that God is more than willing to grant us wisdom if we ask for it, we also must realize that we'll never even scratch the surface of attaining the lofty kind of knowledge and understanding that God has. God and His knowledge are infinite. We are finite. Even if we were as wise and knowledgeable as our own human brains will allow, we would still fall far short of God's knowledge.

While a meteorologist may understand weather patterns and how they operate, it's God who understands weather's inner workings and actually controls the thunder and lightning. People may have the ability to travel to the ends of the earth, but they can never flee from God's presence. The sex of a baby may be determined on a sonogram, but it's God who aligns the chromosomes and knits the child within the mother's womb. The list of mysteries only God fully understands could go on for pages.

When considering all that God knows and regulates on a daily basis, you can't help but be overwhelmed with a sense of newfound awe and wonder about the Creator we serve—the same Creator who performs miracles, answers our prayers, and still has time to meet us right where we are in our time of need. More than just a cliché in Christian circles that made its way into a popular Rich Mullins song: Our God is an awesome God!

We will never be able to fully appreciate just how vast God's knowledge is. When we think about it and are able to catch a glimpse of His infinite wisdom, we should be humbled and comforted by His greatness. We should be humbled because He is so much greater than we could hope to be. We should be comforted to know that the God who loves us also knows us and knows our circumstances.

read →

Now that you've taken the time to consider God's love and wisdom, I suggest you read Brennan Manning's inspiring book *The Wisdom of Tenderness* (Harper San Francisco).

write →

Write about the most compelling, surprising, or intriguing thing you've discovered this week about God's knowledge.

pray →

Thank God for His infinite knowledge, and praise Him that in spite of His all-knowing nature, He still delights in having an open, personal relationship with you.

listen →

Instead of listening to music today, try being quiet and just taking a moment to hear from God. Read Today's Verse again several times. Allow these words—God's words—to speak to your life in a new and fresh way. Read, and listen!

↗ HUNGRY

Introduction

On an episode of *Seinfeld*, the always neurotic but perfectly coiffed Elaine finds herself in a hilarious but precarious position during a job interview.

Executive: Not many people have grace.

Elaine: Well, you know, grace is a tough one. I like to think I have a little grace. Not as much as Jackie O . . .

Executive: You can't have a little grace. You either have grace or you don't.

Elaine: Okay, fine. I have no grace.

Executive: And you can't acquire grace.

Elaine: Well, I have no intention of getting grace.

Executive: Grace isn't something you can pick up at the market.

Elaine: All right, all right, look, I don't have grace, I don't want grace, I don't even say grace, okay?

Executive: Thank you for coming in.

Elaine: Yeah, yeah right.

This scene may represent how confusing the concept of grace can be. Some people see it as a natural endowment given at birth. You either have grace or you don't, and its presence is revealed in how you carry yourself and respond to people. Some people see it as a quality you develop: You may have a "little" grace or a lot. For one person it is an all-or-nothing proposition, while someone else thinks of grace as a formula of words said at the beginning of a meal.

↗HUNGRY

The good news is that God's grace isn't nearly so confusing. He loves us unconditionally and seeks the best for us even though we have sinned against Him and deserve only His wrath. When it comes to God's grace, He has more than just a little that He's willing to supply. In fact, He has enough grace to cover the sin that would separate us from Him for eternity.

Grace is a gift that allows us to have a relationship with Jesus through salvation. While we can't understand why a holy God would love us with such extreme affection despite our inclination to sin, His grace is what distinguishes Christianity from other religions. Rather than earning your way up the ranks, God just moves you right to the top when you surrender your life to have a friendship with Jesus Christ.

Insight: The Elms' Owen Thomas on the grace of God

"I just love constantly being able to remind myself that in all the ways I could let a lot of people down—and they would abandon me for having done so—that's not God. That's not the way God is. I love knowing that God's not at all like me. Whenever I screw somebody over or they let me down enough, I'll walk out on them. But God won't walk out on me. I think I like knowing that God's not like humans. And to try to understand why He would put up with us, it's not even worth doing. It's just knowing that He's capable; that's extremely reassuring to me." (For more about this artist, visit CCMMagazine.com)

Thomas is the frontman for the band, who recently toured with rock legend Peter Frampton at his invitation.

Grace By Definition

today's verse:

"But because of his great love for us, God, who is rich in mercy, made us alive with Christ even when we were dead in transgressions—it is by grace you have been saved."

Ephesians 2:4

Grace is mysterious to us and hard to grasp because it seems to belie everything that we as humans know and hold dear. We're simply not accustomed to something we don't have to earn by making a great first impression, having the right credentials, or working really hard.

Grace is not based on what we do currently, or what we've done in the past. There's no checklist of expectations we have to meet first to gain God's favor. And unlike the best deals in life, it's not a limited-time offer where we have to "act now" to secure our place among "limited" seats. (I would note, however, that the sooner you accept God's grace and His free gift of salvation, the sooner your life will have peace, joy, and purpose like you've never experienced before. But I'll save the details on that for an upcoming study.)

In Luke 15:11-31, Jesus tells a parable that helps illustrate the concept. Basically, there was a man who had two sons. The younger one took his inheritance, left, and quickly squandered his wealth with a wild, partying lifestyle. After his days of excess, a famine hit the land and the younger son found himself struggling for food. When he decides to return home, his father graciously receives him back into the family. The older brother is indignant, however, because he feels the younger brother is no longer worthy to be a son.

This is an astounding parable that reveals at least three important truths: 1) Like the younger son, all of us have sinned against the Father and no longer deserve His grace. 2) Like the older son, we all tend to think we're better than others and aren't all that bad. 3) God—our Father—is infinitely gracious, giving His love to us when it is undeserved.

We will never appreciate God's grace until we recognize how much we're like the younger son. The younger son was rebellious, but he eventually recognized his sin and his need for his father's grace. You can't appreciate the fatted calf until you've been eating with the pigs.

The older son was arrogant and unforgiving. He was loved by the father, but he couldn't appreciate the love because he didn't realize that he was also less than perfect. He felt he had earned his sonship.

Which son are you most like? Do you feel you've been "good" and deserve God's attention and blessing? Or do you recognize your sinful state and your need for God's infinite grace?

read →

For a great additional study on the subject, check out Philip Yancey's classic work *What's So Amazing about Grace?* (Zondervan).

write →

How does reading the story of the prodigal son inspire you? Comment on the grace of God and how you've seen it demonstrated in your life lately.

pray →

In the same way God has extended his unmerited favor toward you, ask Him to give you a similar attitude toward the people in your life who don't seem to deserve it. Make it your goal to see and respond to these people as God would, and expect your thinking to be radically transformed as a result.

listen →

Both **PFR** and **Jars of Clay** have great songs that tie in so perfectly to the subject of grace. Check out PFR's track "Grace of God" from *Great Lengths* (Sparrow) and Jars of Clay's track, simply called "Grace," from *If I Left the Zoo* (Essential).

HUNGRY

HUNGRY

There's No Coach Section in Grace; It's All First-Class!

today's verse:

"For it is by grace that you have been saved, through faith—and this not from yourselves, it is the gift of God—not by works, so that no one can boast."

Ephesians 2:8-9

If you've never had a chance to sit in the first-class section of an airplane before, let me tell you: It's truly an experience you'll never forget. I was always convinced that it was merely a "status thing," but when I got a free upgrade on a business trip because the plane was full, I found out why people enjoy the first-class flying experience. Not only are the seats more comfortable and recline further than any in coach, there's more elbow room; it's quieter; and that particular day they were serving warm chocolate chip cookies.

But before takeoff, when the passengers were walking through, I felt incredibly out of place among the snazzily dressed men and women in business suits. I didn't fit the part, and a few people who passed by me probably even thought, *Now how did she get a seat there?* Don't get me wrong, I wasn't dressed like a bum. But my jeans and sweater hardly fit with the rest of the first-class folks.

In the same way, God's free gift of grace is available to people dressed in suits or jeans. Whether you're a politician or a plumber, grace is obtained in the same fashion. That way, we are almost forced to learn humility.

When Paul wrote today's verse in the book of Ephesians, he was writing from a renewed perspective. With a legalistic background, Paul had bought into the concept that we have to earn our place in heaven by doing as many good works as we can. But after his conversion he was very intentional in his message that eternal life is not contingent on any heavenly scorecard. In fact, he makes a clear distinction that good works are done out of our love for Christ when he says in verse 10, "For we are God's workmanship, created in Christ Jesus to do good works, which God prepared in advance for us to do."

Paul knew what it was like to try earning God's favor by good works. He later discovered what it is like to live under God's grace. For Paul, grace meant moving from coach to First Class! Once you've tasted "the good life" of God's grace, you never want to go back. So it is that everyone today who has found life in Christ is riding in first class. There's no coach section in grace!

HUNGRY

read →

In Ephesians 2:11-22, Paul describes the transition from a life without grace to the life with grace. Read it several times.

write →

Is it difficult for you to concede the idea of salvation not based on works? Are the "good deeds" that you do based out of your love for Christ or a sense of duty? Comment a little about that in the next few lines.

pray →

Ask God what you can do out of your love for Him. Ask Him how your talents can be used to further His kingdom and to share His grace with the world.

insight →

Scotty Smith on grace

"To receive God's grace in Christ is to be bought into a revolutionary reign, not ushered into a quiet rest home! God's love is as disruptive as it is delightful, as demanding as it is delicious! God loves us exactly as we are today, but he loves us too much to leave us as we are and where we are. . . . We who have been made objects of God's tender affection have also been made subjects in his transforming kingdom, servants of the era of 'new creation,' participants in the reign of grace." (For more about this author, visit CCMMagazine.com)

Scotty Smith is a pastor to many of your favorite Christian artists at Christ Community Church in Franklin, Tennessee. His second and most recent book on the subject, The Reign of Grace: The Delights and Demands of God's Love *(Howard), recently released.*

HUNGRY

HUNGRY

Grace on a Daily Basis

today's verse:

"Be wise in the way you act toward outsiders; make the most of every opportunity. Let your conversation be always full of grace, seasoned with salt, so that you may know how to answer everyone."

Colossians 4:5-6

I don't know about you, but I'm a big believer in writing in your Bible. Not just merely highlighting an inspiring verse here or there, but tying the insight from a specific scripture to a situation you're going through and noting that next to the verse.

Now almost five years after my graduation from college, I have the words "Remember Camp Snoopy and Bath & Body Works" next to the verses I've highlighted for today. While it's not exactly relevant now that I live hundreds of miles away from Minneapolis and work at a job I happen to love, recalling that situation convicts me in my daily practice of grace.

While working at Camp Snoopy and Bath & Body Works in college, I was also enrolled in twenty-three credits of classes ("scholastic suicide," I was always told), served as a Sunday school teacher at my church, and was an editor on our campus newspaper, which was my passion at the time. Needless to say, my overcommitment caused me to be less than gracious to a few customers I helped at both of these jobs.

While sometimes people were more than a little slow in the simple process of buying a ticket to ride the roller coaster at Camp Snoopy, or incredibly picky about which Bath & Body Works products to buy for a friend's birthday, they didn't deserve my sarcastic replies to their questions. And I needed to be reminded of that—time and again—so I wrote it down.

Extending grace on a daily basis isn't just for the people you like or who are easy to deal with. How much effort does that require? The real test of grace is when you are willing to give it to people who ridicule you, rub you the wrong way, or just plain annoy you to no end. And if you find it's as difficult for you as it was (and still is sometimes) for me, then you may want to write it down as a constant reminder.

⌐HUNGRY

read →

If you have time to add a little extra reading to your nightstand, *Grace in the First Person: Growing into Life and Faith* by Lee Pearson Knapp (Revell) is a great reflection on today's subject.

write →

In what ways do you struggle with being gracious? When do you find that it's easiest? How can you start being more gracious on a daily basis? Pray about and ponder that today during your journaling time.

pray →

Use the time you've spent writing to fuel your prayer time today.

listen →

"Welcome Home" by **Shaun Groves** from *Invitation to Eavesdrop* (Rocketown); "Grace Flood" by **O.C. Supertones** from *Supertones Strike Back* (BEC).

HUNGRY

HUNGRY

Grace: The Essential Starting Point

today's verse:

"For the grace of God that brings salvation has appeared to all men. It teaches us to say 'No' to ungodliness and worldly passions, and to live self-controlled, upright and godly lives in this present age, while we wait for the blessed hope—the glorious appearing of our great God and Savior, Jesus Christ . . ."

Titus 2:11-13

When people are young, they're usually not as cynical or skeptical because they haven't had enough life experience to become jaded. They haven't had as many people disappoint them yet, and they basically believe that everyone is relatively good and ultimately wants the best for them.

When I accepted Christ at age eleven, that was the worldview I embraced and the mindset I operated under. My father, a new Christian himself at the time, would share the gospel message with me from Romans night after night during our bedtime Bible study. When he told me about salvation, I never wrestled with the concept of God's grace seeming too good to be true. I just accepted it because I saw how having a relationship with Jesus changed my father. And if that's something that changed his life in such a powerfully evident way, I certainly wanted that too. So without any questions or doubt, I prayed the sinner's prayer and my life was miraculously transformed.

Now at twenty-seven—and a lot more cynical based on a variety of life experiences—I often wonder how I would respond to the salvation message if I weren't already a Christian. Would I receive it as readily as before, or would I be more skeptical and have difficulty believing in such a gracious offer? The idea of unmerited favor is something that's hard to grasp in our society where we're inclined to think we have to work as hard as we can to make things happen.

Romans 6:23 reveals that rather than earning God's favor, we have actually earned His judgment as a result of our sin. "For the wages of sin is death, but the gift of God is eternal life in Christ Jesus our Lord." The good news is that while we may have earned death because of our daily transgressions, God freely offers the gift of eternal life to those who believe.

While I've often struggled with not thinking I have much of a "testimony" because I accepted Christ at a young age, I'm so thankful now that I was presented with the concept of God's grace before I became jaded by life's experiences.

HUNGRY

read →

Read through Romans chapter 8. You can't help but be inspired by God's promises for us in those verses.

write →

How did you first come to an understanding of God's grace, and how did that have an impact in your life? Use this time of journaling to reflect on your story and how grace changed the course of your life.

pray →

Take time today to intercede for those who don't yet understand the grace we've been talking about. Aspire to share your faith in a practical way so they may begin to understand.

insight →

Marcus Yoars from Everman on the grace of God

"We are daily reminded of how badly we screw up and how, at the end of the day, we pretty much do nothing right. And the whole concept of grace enters in every morning when you wake up realizing that God still covers us somehow, and despite our faults, despite patterns of sin you're in, God still extends that. That's just constantly blowing our minds lately." (For more about this artist, visit CCMMagazine.com)

Everman is a new piano-based pop/rock band on BEC Records that released its self-titled debut in June 2003.

HUNGRY

HUNGRY

The Sufficiency of Grace

today's verse:

"Let us then approach the throne of grace with confidence, so that we may receive mercy and find grace to help us in our time of need."

Hebrews 4:16

In Hebrews 4:15, we learn more about the Giver of grace than grace itself when it says, "For we do not have a high priest who is unable to sympathize with our weaknesses, but we have one who has been tempted in every way, just as we are—yet was without sin."

Even though we've read those words before, I think we sometimes think that Jesus' time on earth was spent simply blessing people and walking around with a holy air that made Him seem anything but approachable—let alone human. But Jesus was fully man and faced the same kinds of trials and temptations that we encounter on a daily basis. Because of this, Jesus is able to fully understand the challenges we face as human beings.

Jesus wants us to approach His throne with boldness. Whether we need forgiveness from sin or have a physical need that requires immediate attention, He wants us to feel free to come to Him in prayer and receive help exactly when we need it. As we begin to understand His grace and extravagant love for us, we'll desire to improve on our communication with Him. We will begin to regard Him not only as God, but also as our most trusted, loyal friend.

Because God is sovereign (He can do what He wants, when He wants, the way He wants), we can be confident that He is not merely gracious; He is SUFFICIENTLY gracious! It's through the sufficiency of His grace that we'll always be provided for—even in the darkest, most dreadful seasons in our lives. It's there where God's grace is the most evident, and where we usually learn the most about His flawless and loving character.

Have you recognized that God is both sovereign and gracious? Do you realize that He is more than able to provide you with the grace to cover your sins, heal your afflictions, and meet your needs?

HUNGRY

read →

Continuing your reading in Hebrews, backtrack and check out Hebrews 4:12-13 where it talks about the power found in the Word of God. Let these words encourage you as you go about your week.

write →

How has God's grace been sufficient for you this week? Use this time to list a few examples here.

pray →

Take time just to thank God today for His sufficient grace and the fact that He's the truest friend you'll ever have.

insight →

Andrew Peterson on the grace of God

"I'm coming to understand His grace way better now that I have kids. I think that anyone who has kids will tell you that. It's a huge shift in your image of who God is and the way He loves us when you get to love your own child. In the last several years of my life, that's been the most profound experience of grace. I think that part of it is understanding that the grace of God is almost like understanding the difference between just loving your kid and 'loving and liking' your kid. Because God doesn't love us with a love that kind of puts up with you and loves you in that 'I feed you and I clothe you and I take care of you' way the detached parent would do. It's a love that says, 'I like hanging out with you and I like the way you talk and I think it's funny when you do this or you do that.' Understanding the 'like' of God, to me, has almost been as profound an experience as realizing that God loves me at all." (For more about this artist, visit CCMMagazine.com)

Andrew Peterson recently released his third album, Love and Thunder *(Essential), and just wrapped up a tour with Nichole Nordeman.*

↗ HUNGRY

HUNGRY

Grace Is Not Meant to Be Abused

today's verse:

"What shall we say, then? Shall we go on sinning so that grace may increase? By no means! We died to sin; how can we live in it any longer?"

Romans 6:1-2

It may be an old hymn with unfamiliar similes such as "saved a wretch like me," and it may be considered archaic by today's music standards, but there's something very powerful about hearing "Amazing Grace." The chorus gives such a clear picture of where we've been before knowing Christ and where we can be through His generosity.

But what causes theologians and pastors to get a little uncomfortable with such a grace-based faith is our propensity to abuse this amazing gift that we've been given. Embracing grace without also remembering God's call to obedience and holiness is just a greasy form of grace that takes advantage of His kindness toward us and doesn't allow His full work in our lives. Yes, He gives us grace because He loves us unconditionally and so we're able to have an open, thriving friendship with Christ. But that does not provide us with a license to sin.

Our desire to not want to abuse the grace He's given us should come out of our love for God and reverence for the miracles He's performed in our lives. If you love your boyfriend/girlfriend or husband/wife, you wouldn't want to deliberately do something you know would break his or her heart, would you? If you really love that person, of course you wouldn't. In the same way, our love for God should make us more aware of our sin and the motives behind why we fall short; it should also cause us not to want to sin because it grieves His heart. That doesn't mean that we're not going to fail and need His forgiveness. But our hearts should be in a condition where we listen to the voice of the Holy Spirit, reject sin and the evil that tempts us, and live in the fullness of the grace He's given us.

So, in the end it is all about our relationship with Jesus. His grace forgives us and draws us into a personal relationship with Him. That relationship, in turn, motivates us to live in a way that honors the One who first loved us. As our love for Him grows, we learn more and more about what pleases Him and we increasingly avoid sin, not because we have to, but because we want to.

HUNGRY

read →

Read the rest of Romans 6 where it elaborates on the issue of grace and how we are dead to sin and alive in Christ.

write →

Now that you've been learning about the attribute of God's grace for the past six days, write a little about the most compelling, surprising, or intriguing thing you've discovered about God as a result.

pray →

Ask God to reveal to you where you've taken advantage of His grace. Now, this isn't easy stuff to hear, but asking Him enables you to know your weaknesses so you don't trip up the next time. Give thanks for these revelations and also thank Him for his unchanging grace that saves sinners like us every day.

listen →

Since we referenced an old hymn today already, I'm suggesting another musical selection from a more vintage catalog as well. Check out the late **Keith Green**'s powerful songs "Your Love Broke Thru" and "Because of You" from *Keith Green: The Ministry Years I* (Sparrow).

HUNGRY